Lu

by Lynn Edwards
illustrated by Kersti Frigell

SRA McGraw-Hill

Columbus, Ohio

A Division of The McGraw-Hill Companies

SRA/McGraw-Hill
*A Division of The **McGraw·Hill** Companies*

Copyright © 1998 by SRA/McGraw-Hill.

All rights reserved. Except as permitted under the United States Copyright Act, no part of this publication may be reproduced or distributed in any form or by any means, or stored in a database or retrieval system, without prior written permission from the publisher.

Printed in the United States of America.

Send all inquiries to:
SRA/McGraw-Hill
250 Old Wilson Bridge Road
Suite 310
Worthington, OH 43085

ISBN 0-02-674287-X

2 3 4 5 6 7 8 9 SEG 00 99 98 97

Here is a  .

Here is a  .

sandwich

Here is an 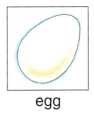 .
egg

Here is an .

Here is a  .

Here is  .

lunch